The Blackbirch Visual Encyclopedia

World History

BLACKBIRCH®
PRESS

THOMSON
★
GALE

San Diego • Detroit • New York • San Francisco • Cleveland • New Haven, Conn. • Waterville, Maine • London • Munich

CONTENTS

THOMSON
GALE

© 2002 by Blackbirch Press™. Blackbirch Press™ is an imprint of The Gale Group, Inc., a division of Thomson Learning, Inc.

Blackbirch Press™ and Thomson Learning™ are trademarks used herein under license.

For more information, contact
The Gale Group, Inc.
27500 Drake Rd.
Farmington Hills, MI 48331-3535
Or you can visit our Internet site at http://www.gale.com

Copyright © 2000 Orpheus Books Ltd. Created and produced by Nicholas Harris, Joanna Turner, and Claire Aston, Orpheus Books Ltd.

Text credit: Nicola Barber

Consultant credit: Dr. Robert Peberdy

Illustration credit: Simone Boni, Stephen Conlin, Giuliano Fornari, Luigi Galante, Andrea Ricciardi di Gaudesi, Gary Hincks, Steve Noon, Nicki Palin, Alessandro Rabatti, Claudia Saraceni, Sergio, Thomas Trojer, Alan Weston

Photographs on pages 41, 45, 49, 50, 51, 52, 54, 55, 56: The Illustrated London News Picture Library.
Photograph on page 34: National Gallery, London

LIBRARY OF CONGRESS CATALOGING-IN-PUBLICATION DATA

Harris, Nicholas, 1956-
World history / Nicholas Harris.
  p. cm. — (Blackbirch visual encyclopedia)
  Includes index.
  Summary: A visual encyclopedia of significant places and events in world history from the Middle Ages through the twentieth century.
  ISBN 1-56711-520-9 (lib. bdg. : alk. paper)
  1. World history—Juvenile literature [1. World history—Encyclopedias.] I. Title. II. Series.

D23 .H295 2002
909—dc21   2002018654

Printed in Singapore
10 9 8 7 6 5 4 3 2 1

CONTENTS

MIDDLE AGES

THE ARAB WORLD

IN ABOUT 570 the prophet Muhammad was born in the city of Mecca in Arabia. He was orphaned as a young boy. When he was about 12 years old, the prophet Muhammad began work as a trader for his uncle and soon became known for his honesty. He married the widow of a wealthy merchant and became a successful businessman. When he was about 40, the prophet Muhammad began to go to the mountains outside Mecca to be by himself and think. It was here that the angel Gabriel came to him with a message from Allah (God). Gabriel told him that people should worship one God, Allah, and only Allah. The prophet Muhammad began to preach Gabriel's message to the people of Makkah. The appearances of Gabriel to the prophet Muhammad marked the beginning of the Islamic faith. Followers became known as Muslims. Muslims believe that there is only one God, Allah, and that the prophet Muhammad was the last messenger (prophet) of Allah. They believe that the messages given to the prophet Muhammad by Gabriel were the words of Allah. These were eventually brought together to form the holy book of Islam, the Qur'an (Koran).

Arab warriors attack on horseback, armed with spears, bows and arrows, and swords. The Arabs bred highly prized horses for use in battle. They also used camels to cross dry and inhospitable desert regions where horses would not survive.

By the early 14th century, gunpowder was being imported from China, and the Arabs quickly learned how to make it for themselves. At first they used it to fire arrows from simple guns. More complicated guns and cannons soon became an important part of warfare in the Arab world.

THE SPREAD OF ISLAM

By the time of the death of the prophet Muhammad in 632, the Islamic faith was already spreading throughout Arabia. Within 25 years, Arab armies had taken control of parts of the mighty Byzantine (see page 7) and Sassanian Empires, including what is now Syria, Iraq, Iran, and Egypt. Islam quickly spread to these lands.

UMAYYADS AND ABBASIDS

Muslims across the expanding Islamic empire were united by their faith, their belief in Allah and their respect for the Qur'an. The leader of the Islamic community was known as the caliph (meaning "successor"). In 661 the first caliph of the Umayyad clan came to power as leader of the Islamic world. The Umayyad dynasty held on to power until 750, when the Abbasids seized control. Under the Umayyads, the Islamic faith reached as far west as Spain, and deep into central Asia in the east. Arabic was made the official language throughout the empire.

The Alhambra palace in Granada, Spain was built by the Moors, the Muslims who ruled part of Spain from the 700s to 1492. The Alhambra gets its name from the Arabic word for "red", because of the red brick used to build the outer walls.

The Abbasids built a fabulous new city to be the administrative center of their empire. Founded in 762, Baghdad (in present-day Iraq) attracted scholars, artists, and crafts-people from all parts of the empire. It became a center for learning and the arts. The most famous of the Abbasid caliphs was Harun al-Rashid (governed 786–809) whose court was the setting for the *Thousand and One Nights*, a collection of stories from Arabia, China, Egypt, and India.

Baghdad was a busy trade center. Goods came from as far as India and China.

THE BARBARIANS

THE WORD *barbarian* originally came from the ancient Greeks, who used it to describe anyone who spoke a language they could not understand—a foreigner. The Romans applied the word to the peoples outside their vast empire—for example, the Huns, Goths, and Vandals. It was these barbarians who finally brought an end to the Roman Empire.

ATTACKS ON ROME

The Goths and Vandals were Germanic tribes who came originally from southern Scandinavia. The Huns originated from central Asia. Sometime after 370 the Huns attacked eastern Europe, threatening the Goths, who moved to the west and to the south. Under their leader Attila, the Huns went on to attack Gaul (France), a land controlled by Rome, although they were defeated following the death of Attila in 453. Meanwhile, the Goths invaded Italy itself, looting Rome in 410.

The Vandals moved across Gaul and Spain to invade northern Africa in 429. They took

In 800 Charlemagne was crowned emperor of the lands he ruled over, now known as the Holy Roman Empire.

over the Roman provinces there and established a kingdom. From this base they sacked Rome in 455.

The Franks were another Germanic people. Under their leader, Clovis, they took over Gaul in the early 6th century. Clovis was the first Germanic ruler to adopt Christianity. Another famous Frankish king, Charlemagne, ruled from 768 to 814 and built up a massive empire *(see map above)*.

King Alaric leads his Gothic army into Rome in 410.

BYZANTIUM

WHILE THE western half of the Roman Empire collapsed, overrun by Germanic tribes, the eastern half continued to thrive. In 330 the Roman emperor Constantine I had founded a new capital at Byzantium, a city-port on the European side of the Bosporus strait. This capital was renamed Constantinople, and it became the flourishing center of the eastern half of the Roman Empire, which was known as the Byzantine Empire. Under the influence of Constantine and his son Theodosius I, Christianity was the official religion of the Byzantine Empire and Constantinople the Christian capital of the East.

JUSTINIAN

The greatest of the emperors that ruled the Byzantine Empire was Justinian (reigned 527–65). Under Justinian, the Byzantine Empire expanded to its greatest size. The Byzantine armies, under their commander Belisarius, reconquered much of the land lost from the Roman Empire in North Africa, Greece, Turkey, Italy, and parts of

This is a mosaic portrait of Justinian. A mosaic is made up of hundreds of pieces of painted marble.

Spain. Justinian is remembered for his legal and administrative skills. He tried to stamp out injustice and corruption in his empire, issuing a code of laws that has since been used to form the basis for legal systems in many countries. It was also during Justinian's reign that the Byzantines built the magnificent church of Hagia Sophia in Constantinople, with its massive dome, beautiful wall paintings, and golden, glittering mosaics.

During Byzantine times, hundreds of caves and churches were carved out of strange rock formations found in Cappadocia, Turkey. They still exist today.

INVASION AND CONQUEST

The conquests of Justinian's reign used up nearly all the empire's funds, and even before the emperor's death, barbarian tribes were reconquering parts of the empire in the west. After 565 the Byzantine Empire was never as powerful again. A new enemy appeared in the 7th century as Arab armies began to invade after the death of Muhammad in 632 (see page 4). The Arabs quickly took control of the empire's territories in the Middle East. The Byzantine Empire flourished once more in the late 9th century under the rule of Basil I. But after the 11th century, the empire was weakened by further invasions, and it finally came to an end when Constantinople fell to the Turks in 1453.

CHINA

THE HAN dynasty ruled China for about 400 years, until the defeat of the last Han emperor in A.D. 220. During this time, the empire had expanded into central Asia, and trade had flourished along the Silk Road, linking China with the West. But the end of the Han dynasty brought confusion to China as nomads attacked from the north and the country split into three kingdoms. China was reunited again by the brief rule of the Sui dynasty (581–618).

During the Yuan (Mongol) dynasty, European interest in China increased as reports of the riches that lay in the East were brought back by travelers and traders. One of these travelers was Marco Polo, who set off from Venice in 1271 when he was 17 years old. He journeyed with his father, Niccolo, and uncle, Matteo, across Asia. He traveled widely in China from 1275 to 1292, visiting the palace of the great Mongol emperor, Kublai Khan *(see pages 14–15)* in 1274. On his return home he wrote an account of his amazing experiences—although almost no one believed him.

THE TANG DYNASTY

The Tang dynasty came to power when Li Yuan seized power in 618. This dynasty lasted until 907, and it was a time of great prosperity. Sea trade grew, and many ports became bustling centers of commerce. The Tang capital Changan (present-day Xi'an) attracted scholars, artists, and poets from all parts of Asia. The Buddhist religion became increasingly important, and many shrines and temples were built.

The Song dynasty was a period of great inventiveness in Chinese history. This mechanical water clock was built in 1029 by Su Song, and it ran for nearly 50 years. Other inventions included gunpowder and movable type, used for printing.

LATER DYNASTIES

After a period of civil war, the Song dynasty began in 960. Once again, this was a time of peace and prosperity in China, which was probably the wealthiest country in the world during the 11th and 12th centuries. An improved type of rice meant that food production increased, and the population of China topped 100 million. However, there was the constant threat from nomadic tribes to the north, and during the 1200s, the Mongols swept into China *(see pages 14-15)*. Under their leader, Kublai Khan, they established the Mongol, or Yuan, dynasty.

Kublai Khan established a new capital at Beijing and improved the road system in his new empire. But the Mongols ruled harshly and, after Kublai Khan's death, rebellions eventually drove the Mongols out of China. In 1368 the Ming emperors took control. The Ming tried to keep foreign influences out of China, severely restricting the activities of European merchants in their country. However, the Ming were overpowered in 1644 by more foreigners—the Manchus from Manchuria. They established the Qing dynasty and quickly adopted Chinese ways of life and culture. They ruled until 1912.

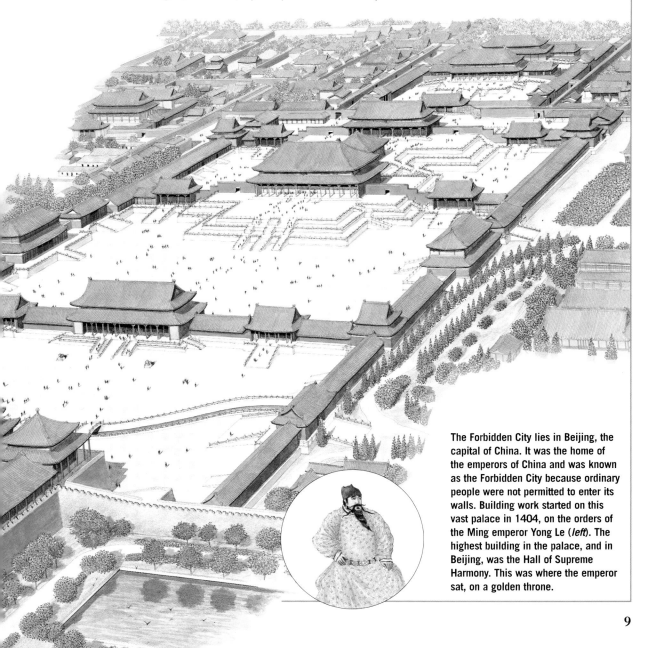

The Forbidden City lies in Beijing, the capital of China. It was the home of the emperors of China and was known as the Forbidden City because ordinary people were not permitted to enter its walls. Building work started on this vast palace in 1404, on the orders of the Ming emperor Yong Le (*left*). The highest building in the palace, and in Beijing, was the Hall of Supreme Harmony. This was where the emperor sat, on a golden throne.

Maya and Aztecs

BOTH THE Maya and the Aztecs had powerful civilizations in Central America. The Maya inhabited the Yucatán Peninsula *(see map below),* and their civilization reached the height of its power from the 3rd to the 10th centuries A.D. The Aztec's mighty empire lay in what is now Mexico. It was based around the capital city, Tenochtitlán (on the site of present-day Mexico City). The Aztecs flourished for about 100 years, from the 1400s to 1521.

An Aztec jaguar knight wore the skins, head, jaws, and teeth of a jaguar. These jaguar knights were the finest Aztec warriors and they were highly respected.

Both the Maya and Aztecs held power in Central America. The Maya civilization covered a region that lies in present-day Mexico, Guatemala, Honduras, and El Salvador. The Aztec civilization lay farther west. The Incas had a vast empire in South America that stretched more than 1,243 miles (2,000 km) down the Pacific coast. They held power in the 14th and 15th centuries *(see page 29).*

The Maya

The Maya civilization was built around city-states. The Maya built great cities, such as Tikal, each of which controlled its surrounding area and sometimes other smaller and less important cities, too. Important trade routes connected the city-states, as well as linking the Maya with other peoples in Central America. Goods for trade included jaguar skins, jade, salt, and cacao beans. The Maya transported goods by river and sea, or overland by foot.

In the countryside, most Maya people were farmers. One of the most important crops was maize which was used to make a type of flat bread, called tortilla, and an alcoholic drink called *balche.*

The Maya became very advanced in branches of astronomy and mathematics. Maya priests used this knowledge to draw up a calendar. The Maya also developed a writing system that used many different symbols. They kept records on large stone monuments known as stelae.

The Maya civilization came to an end when Spanish conquerors invaded in the 1500s. Descendants of the Maya continue to live in the region, speaking Mayan languages.

Both the Aztecs and the Maya built their temples in the shape of stepped pyramids, some as high as 147.6 miles (45 m). Many of these temples were used to sacrifice human victims. Captives were led to the altars at the top of a temple and killed in a bloody ritual.

Ball games were very popular. In this Aztec game, two players tried to knock a ball through a ring. They were allowed to use only their forearms, hips, and thighs to touch the ball. It was serious sport—members of the losing team were often sacrificed to the gods.

much of the land surrounding the city. Under their ruler Montezuma I (ruled 1440-68), the Aztecs extended their empire. When Montezuma II became emperor in 1502, the empire was at its height. Then, in 1519, Spanish invaders (*see page 33*) attacked the Aztecs. The spears and clubs of the fierce Aztec warriors were no match for Spanish guns and by 1521 the empire was defeated.

Religion was very important in the lives of both the Maya and the Aztecs. Both peoples worshiped many gods. They held religious ceremonies at which human sacrifices were made to ensure plentiful harvests and good fortune.

THE AZTECS

The center of the Aztec civilization was Tenochtitlán, the capital. Founded in 1325, the city covered about 5.8 square miles (15 km²) and was built on an island in Lake Texcoco. By the 1400s, the Aztecs controlled

Today only ruins remain of the great Maya city of Chichén Itzá. The city grew to become one of the most powerful Maya centers between 900 and 1200.

THE VIKINGS

THE VIKINGS were seafaring peoples who came from the Scandinavian countries of northern Europe (modern-day Denmark, Norway, and Sweden). Between about 750 and 1100, the Vikings raided and looted many parts of Europe. They were also colonizers, founding settlements in many regions including Iceland and Greenland. Viking ships even sailed as far west as North America. Five hundred years before Christopher Columbus made his historic voyage across the Atlantic Ocean *(see page 32)*, a Viking named Leif Ericsson landed on the coast of North America, probably in Newfoundland. He was the first European to set foot on North American soil. Ericsson established a settlement, but it was abandoned after a few years.

Along the Atlantic coastline of Scandinavia the sea cuts into the shoreline, creating deep inlets, and it is thought that the name Viking comes from the word *vik* meaning "inlet." The Vikings were also known as Norsemen (or Northmen) by the peoples who feared their raids. As well as being fearsome warriors, the Vikings were great traders, sailing as far south as the Mediterranean Sea to exchange farm products and furs for weapons and luxury items such as gold, silver, and silk.

VIKING RAIDERS

The Vikings carried out raids across much of Europe, from England to Italy, Russia to Spain. But what made the Vikings sail across the seas to attack towns and villages? One reason was a large increase in population in the Viking homelands which led to overcrowding and a shortage of farmland. Many Vikings decided to leave Scandinavia to look for new land elsewhere—even if they had to fight for it. Another reason was that the Vikings were naturally adventurous, and many young warriors saw raiding as a way of gaining wealth and honor. They favored surprise attacks, and they looted everything from cattle and horses to valuable objects stolen from churches and monasteries. They showed little mercy to the terrified populations, and what they did not steal, they usually burned.

Viking raiders on board a longship. Shields were placed along the sides of the ship.

This noble Viking warrior has two weapons—a sword and a spear. He is also carrying a wooden shield for protection. His helmet is made from iron and he wears a chain mail tunic around his body. Only wealthy Viking leaders wore such metal armor.

HOME LIFE

Most Vikings were farmers. In forested Scandinavia they lived in timber houses, but in places where wood was scarce they used stone instead. They grew crops such as barley, oats, and rye and kept cattle, goats, sheep and pigs. Some Vikings worked as fishermen, catching freshwater and sea fish as well as hunting for whales. Salt was a vital commodity, usually bought from traveling merchants. It was used to preserve fish and meat for the long winters.

The clothes of the Vikings were simple and practical, made from woolen or linen

A Viking fortress *(below)* was protected by circular embankments of wood and soil. There were four entrances to the fort.

VIKING SHIPS

The Vikings were some of the most skilful boatbuilders and sailors of their time. Their ships, known as longships or dragon ships, were sleek and fast. A longship was built from wood and had a keel—a strip of wood that ran the length of the ship and cut into the water, helping to reduce the rolling motion. It was powered by a square-shaped sail or, if there was no wind, by oarsmen. The front end was often carved into an ornamental shape, such as a dragon's head.

cloth. Men wore trousers and a long-sleeved shirt, women wore loose-fitting dresses. Both men and women wore leather shoes.

The Vikings had a system of writing, called runes. Viking history, however, was not written but passed down the generations by word of mouth in verse stories called sagas. The Vikings were also skilful woodcarvers and metalworkers. They decorated their ships and houses with intricate carvings and wore beautiful jewelry, much of it made from silver.

The Vikings fought with axes, spears, swords, and bows and arrows. Highly prized by Viking warriors, swords *(right)* often had highly decorated handles. The blades were made of iron or steel. Ornate brooches *(far right)* were often worn on cloaks.

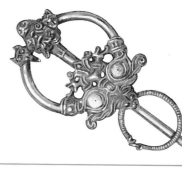

THE MONGOLS

THE MONGOLS were a nomadic people who lived on the steppes of central Asia, from the Ural Mountains to the Gobi desert. They moved from place to place with their herds of sheep, goats, and cattle, and they were skilful and daring on horseback. The Mongol peoples lived in tents made from felt, called yurts. Besides providing good protection, they were also easy to take down and put up again.

GENGHIS KHAN

The Mongols were fierce warriors, and members of one tribe often raided another tribe to accumulate wealth and prestige. However, in about 1200, a Mongol leader named Temüjin rose to power and brought all the Mongol tribes under his control.

Temüjin became known as Genghis Khan. Under his rule the Mongols attacked northern China as well as the lands that lay to the west. The Mongol armies rampaged across Russia and came within reach of Constantinople (see page 7). Everywhere they went, the Mongols inspired terror as they looted, destroyed, and slaughtered without mercy.

KUBLAI KHAN

When Genghis Khan died in China in 1227 the empire passed to his four sons. One, Ögödei, dominated the rest and continued his father's campaigns in Europe. Ögödei was killed in 1241 and, after much feuding, a grandson of Genghis Khan, Kublai Khan, eventually achieved power in 1264. He was determined to conquer all of China, and he finally succeeded in 1279.

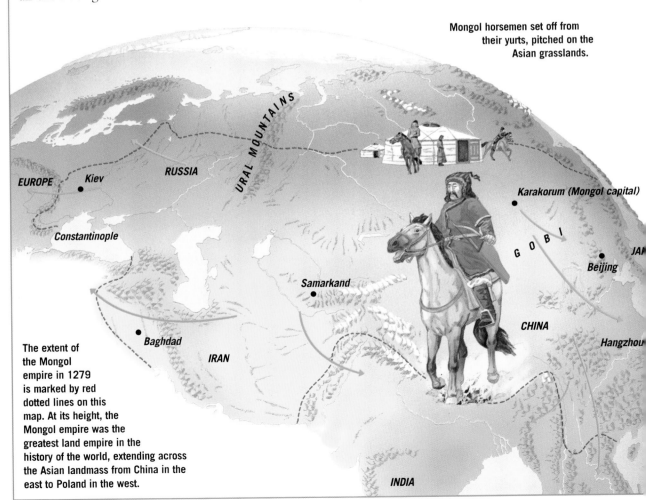

Mongol horsemen set off from their yurts, pitched on the Asian grasslands.

EUROPE · Kiev   RUSSIA   URAL MOUNTAINS   Karakorum (Mongol capital)

Constantinople   GOBI   JA[

Samarkand   Beijing

· Baghdad   CHINA   Hangzhou

IRAN

The extent of the Mongol empire in 1279 is marked by red dotted lines on this map. At its height, the Mongol empire was the greatest land empire in the history of the world, extending across the Asian landmass from China in the east to Poland in the west.

INDIA

Genghis Khan was born in either 1162 or 1167. His early life was one of poverty, existing on roots, nuts, and berries. We know about his life from the Mongol chronicle, the *Secret History of the Mongols,* which was written in about 1240. He was the first leader to bring the Mongols together as one nation, and to organize the Mongol armies in large-scale and successful campaigns.

MONGOL RULE

Kublai Khan was a tolerant ruler. He permitted the existence of various religions in China, including Buddhism, Islam, and Christianity. He organized food stores for times of famine, and he improved the road system so that trade could increase. He also tried to extend Mongol power to Japan, but his fleets were defeated in 1274 and 1281.

The heavy cavalry of the Mongol army was made up of armored horses and riders like this one. The nobleman's helmet and armor were made mostly of leather.

A Mongol archer prepares to loose a fatal arrow *(below).* Early in an attack, Mongol archers fired light arrows. When the enemy was at closer range, they used heavier, armor-piercing arrows. Every archer carried a bow and two quivers, containing about 30 arrows in total. Their short bows were specially designed to fire arrows with great power and accuracy.

THE END OF THE EMPIRE

After the death of Kublai Khan in 1294, his mighty empire began to decline. By 1368 the Chinese had overthrown their Mongol rulers. However, in the central Asian city of Samarkand, a descendant of Genghis Khan named Tamerlane (also Timur the Lame) seized the throne in 1369. He extended his power to the south and to the west, invading India in 1398. Tamerlane's troops sacked Delhi and killed most of its inhabitants. Nevertheless, after his death in 1405, Tamerlane's empire quickly fell apart. In 1526 one of Tamerlane's descendants became the first Great Mughal, ruler of the Mughal empire in India *(see page 39).*

JAPAN

IN THE 5TH CENTURY, Japan was a remote land. Few people from the outside world ever visited this group of islands. But after about 550, Japan began to fall under the influence of its much larger neighbor, China. Buddhist monks from China persuaded the Japanese emperor to adopt Buddhism as the national religion. Scholars taught the Japanese to read and write Chinese. Prince Shotoku (574–622) was an enthusiastic follower of Buddhism and founded many temples in Japan. He also

A pagoda is a tower with several stories. All pagodas are said to contain a relic of Buddha (something used by or associated with him). Rebuilt after after a fire in 670, the Horyuji pagoda survives to this day.

Samurai warriors wore armor made of metal plates. For weapons they used swords, lances, and bows and arrows. The samurai's bow was taller than a man and fired arrows sharp enough to penetrate metal armor.

organized the system of government in Japan along Chinese lines, concentrating power on the emperor himself. By 800 the Japanese way of life was very similar to that of China.

In 858 a powerful man called Fujiwara Yoshifusa became regent for a nine-year-old emperor. He was supposed to rule Japan only while the emperor was a child, but he continued in power as a dictator even after the emperor became an adult. For many centuries after that, Japan was ruled by powerful military men. Wars broke out between rival clans bidding for power. The Fujiwara clan lost out to the Taira, who in turn were defeated by the Minamoto. Minamoto Yoritomo took on the title of shogun (great general) in 1192.

Prince Shotoku built the Horyuji, Japan's oldest surviving Buddhist monastery, between 601 and 607, at the city of Nara.

THE SAMURAI

During shogun rule, a powerful force in Japan were the samurai. These warrior knights enforced law and order in the land on behalf of local lords (daimyo) and were on hand to fight for the shogun if called upon. Samurai warriors followed a code of honor known as the Bushido. The samurai were summoned to fight the Mongol armies that invaded Japan in 1274 (see page 15). The Mongol fleet was destroyed in a storm, but a new, even larger invasion was mounted in 1281. This time, a typhoon (hurricane) devastated the Mongol force and Japan was saved. The Japanese called these storms kamikaze ("divine winds").

The daimyo, together with his family and soldiers, lived in hilltop castles dominated by a building called a tenshu. This is Himeji Castle, known as the White Heron.

CIVIL WARS

Rivalry between clans continued, and some powerful daimyo became too powerful for the shogun to control. Wars frequently broke out between them from the 14th to 16th centuries, the fiercest being the Onin War, which lasted from 1467 to 1477. Eventually, unity was restored to the country and Toyotomi Hideyoshi became undisputed master of all Japan in 1591. The Tokugawa family took over in 1603. Nearly all trade and contact between Japan and foreign nations closed down for more than 200 years.

KHMER KINGDOM

CHINESE RULERS, or local leaders loyal to China, once governed Southeast Asia. But from the 3rd century AD, traders and religious men from India introduced Hinduism and Buddhism to the local inhabitants. In Cambodia, Chinese rule was shaken off in the 9th century when the Khmer Kingdom was founded.

The building of a new capital city, called Angkor, which would grow into a vast complex of temples and houses for one million people, was begun in about 900. The temples, many of whose sandstone walls were covered by beautiful carvings of god-kings, dancers, and animals, were surrounded by a network of dams and irrigation channels.

The Khmer Kingdom was finally overrun by armies of the neighboring Thai kingdom in the mid–15th century. Angkor was abandoned to the jungle and not rediscovered until 1861 when a French naturalist, Albert Henri Mouhot, came across it by accident.

One of Angkor's many magnificent temples, called Angkor Wat, was built by King Suryavarman II (ruled 1113-50) as a palace and shrine to the god-king himself. A flight of steps leads up to the summit of the central "temple mountain," topped by five lotus-bud towers.

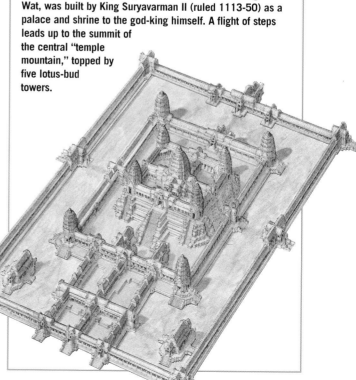

MEDIEVAL EUROPE

IN EUROPE, the period from about A.D. 500 to 1500 is known as the Middle Ages, or the medieval period. The Middle Ages began after the collapse of the Roman Empire *(see page 6)* and ended with the start of the Renaissance *(see page 34)*. The early part of this period was a time of invasions, including Viking raids *(see pages 12–13)* and the conquest of England by Duke William of Normandy in 1066. The later part saw frequent wars between the kingdoms that covered Europe, including the so-called Hundred Years' War fought between England and France (1337–1453).

THE FEUDAL SYSTEM

The feudal system, or feudalism, is the term used to describe a political and military system that developed in Europe during the Middle Ages. It had its roots with the Franks *(see page 6),* when Frankish warriors pledged loyalty to a ruler or lord in return for some sort of protection and reward. Feudalism spread across Europe between the 800s and 1200s. In return for military or other services, a lord would reward a loyal follower, known as a vassal. The reward was often in the form of land. The vassal was given the use of the land, although he did not own it. In return, he promised loyalty.

Noble vassals divided up the land given to them by their lord or king into manors *(right)*. The land in each manor was worked by peasants. As well as laboring in their lord's fields, the peasants had small plots or strips of land on which to grow their own food. Some manors also had a windmill for grinding grain into flour.

Market day at a town in medieval Europe *(below, left)*. Markets were very important in the Middle Ages. Farmers brought their produce to sell to the townspeople. Travelling merchants sold fine cloth to wealthy people. Jugglers entertained the crowds.

In the uncertain times experienced by people across Europe during the early Middle Ages, feudalism provided some kind of security and protection. But by the late 1200s, the system was beginning to fall apart. People began to make more use of money, preferring to pay rent for land than be bound by the feudal system. Lords, too, could pay for soldiers rather than reward them with land.

THE DOMESDAY BOOK

In early 1086 William I (the Conqueror) ordered a survey of the whole of England. After his victory of 1066, he wanted information about his kingdom. The result was a place-by-place survey of the whole of England (except for London, Winchester, and parts of northern England), listing population, wealth, and who owned what. It was later called the Domesday Book. Similar surveys were also made elsewhere in Europe from the 12th century onwards.

Such detailed work required people who could read and write, and it was during the Middle Ages that the earliest universities were founded in Europe—for example, in the Italian town of Bologna (1088).

THE BLACK DEATH

The Black Death was a terrible disease that killed millions of people in Europe in the 1340s. The name might have come from the black spots that appeared on victims. The disease came from Asia in 1347 and spread across Europe in the following years. It was carried by fleas that lived on black rats—although no one knew that at the time.

No one in the Middle Ages understood where the Black Death came from or how to treat it. Many people died within a day of catching the disease. The dead bodies were collected on carts. People fled from infected towns —spreading the disease as they went.

TRADE AND FAITH

BEFORE THE YEARS of plague *(see page 19)* and famine in the 1300s, medieval Europe was an increasingly wealthy place. Across Europe, land was drained and forests were cut down to bring more land under cultivation. In some places this process happened as villages expanded. In other places, fortresses were built as defense against invaders, or monasteries were founded in remote places, providing the starting-points for new settlements.

As the amount of food production increased so did the population. In 1000 it is estimated that the population of Europe was about 40 million. It rose dramatically to about 80 million in 1300, falling again in the 1300s as a result of plague and famine.

Any increase in wealth usually went to the lord of the manor, but life changed little for the peasants in the fields. They continued to live in cramped and disease-ridden conditions, with a monotonous diet of coarse bread, porridge, and vegetables. They very rarely ate fish or meat. These were delicacies reserved for the table of the lord of the manor.

This is the Hölstentor Gate in the German town of Lübeck, one of the members of the Hanseatic League.

THE HANSEATIC LEAGUE

Towns were important centers of growth between 1000 and 1300 in Europe, particularly those on the great trading routes. In Germany, several towns joined together to form a trade alliance known as the Hanseatic League. The towns of the league gained control of the trade in furs, fish and timber in northern Europe. Further south on the Mediterranean Sea, Italian cities such as Venice and Genoa became

People of the Middle Ages: *(from left to right)* a merchant, a lady of the royal court, a falconer, a friar, and a peasant. Both the court lady and the merchant wear rich clothing while the peasant woman is much more simply dressed. The falconer would have worked at court or for the lord of the manor. Falconry was very popular in Europe in the Middle Ages and was known as the sport of kings. Falcons, hawks, and eagles were all trained to hunt. The falconer wore a heavy glove to protect his hand when the bird perched on it. The friar was a monk who did not live inside a monastery. Instead he traveled from place to place, preaching Christianity as he went. In medieval feudal society, the nobility held all the wealth and power. Below them came merchants and craftspeople. Peasants and servants were the poorest people.

centers for trade with Asia and North Africa. Many of these exotic wares—silks, spices, and sugar—were then transported across the alpine passes for sale in northern Europe. In the other direction, wool, iron, and furs were taken southwards.

THE CHRISTIAN CHURCH

The Christian Church became very powerful during the Middle Ages in Europe. Christianity was an important part of everyday life for everyone—from peasant to lord. Many men and women chose to devote their lives to the church by becoming monks or nuns. They lived in monasteries or nunneries and also worked in the fields or looked after the poor and the sick. They also spent much of their time in prayer and study, copying texts and decorating them with beautiful pictures and letters, called illuminations. As a result, monasteries and nunneries became centers of scholarship across Europe.

There were several orders (organizations) of monks and nuns. The earliest was started by St. Benedict of Nursia who founded the Benedictine order in the 500s. St. Benedict was the author of the Rule—a set of guidelines for monastic life.

Thousands of monasteries, abbeys, churches, and cathedrals were constructed across Europe during the Middle Ages. The largest took many years to complete. Some of the largest abbeys, for example Cluny in France, were like small, self-contained towns within their own walls.

Many magnificent cathedrals were built during the Middle Ages in Europe. The word *cathedral* comes from *cathedra*, meaning "bishop's throne". A cathedral was the building where the bishop's throne was kept.

Knights on horseback set off for battle during the Crusades.

KNIGHTS

WHEN WILLIAM I (the Conqueror) invaded England in 1066 he brought with him mounted soldiers. They were called *cnihts* by the English, a word meaning "servant" or "retainer." Under the feudal system, many of these soldiers became vassals *(see page 18),* and the word *knight* soon came to describe someone who served a king or lord as a mounted and armed soldier. Knights became a separate class of people, below the higher nobility in the feudal system but above merchants and craftspeople. Knights were expected to follow a code of loyalty and honor and to protect the weak. This was known as the code of chivalry.

BECOMING A KNIGHT

Boys destined to become knights went through years of training. This was necessary to learn the fighting skills and the code of chivalrous behavior expected of a knight. Young boys were sent as pages to live in a knight's household. At the age of 15 or 16, a page became a squire, acting as the personal servant to a knight. A squire rode into battle with his master and learned how to fight. When this training was complete, the squire was ready to become a knight. This took place at a dubbing ceremony *(see opposite).*

A knight took various weapons into battle. His main weapon was his lance, a long pole used to unseat other riders. He also carried a sword, mace, and battle-ax.

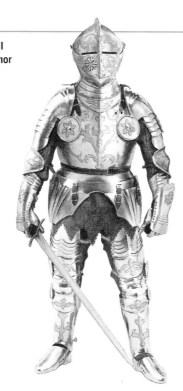

A knight dressed in full armor. This type of armor dates from the 15th century, when knights wore heavy suits made from metal plates weighing up to 55.12 lbs. (25 kilos). Dressed in this armor, knights had to be lifted on to their horses with a crane. If they fell off, they were helpless. Hidden by his armor, the only way to recognize a knight was by the coat of arms on his shield.

A squire becomes a knight in the dubbing ceremony. The squire kneels before his master or the king to receive a light tap on the shoulder with a sword, accompanied by the words "I dub you knight."

THE CRUSADES

In 1095 Pope Urban II, the leader of the Christian Church, called for European Christians to stop fighting among themselves and instead to recapture Palestine, the Holy Land. This region was important to Christians because it was where Jesus Christ had lived. In the 1000s it had been captured by the Turks, who made it difficult for Christians to visit holy sites and shrines. In 1095 the Turks had banned Christians from entering Jerusalem.

In answer to the Pope's call, Christians from all over Europe organized military expeditions called Crusades. There were eight Crusades in all (1096-1270). The aim of the crusaders was to recapture the Holy Land and to protect the Byzantine Empire *(see page 7)* from the Turks.

Everyone from kings to knights, nobles to peasants took part in the Crusades. In 1212 there was even a Children's Crusade when thousands of boys and girls set off across Europe on the long trek south to the Mediterranean. Many of them perished.

The crusaders failed to win back the Holy Land, and the Turks captured the Byzantine Empire in 1453. But trade and other contacts between Europe and Asia flourished as a result of the Crusades.

Two knights take part in a tournament, watched by a crowd of nobles. These knights are tilting. The purpose of tilting was to unseat the opposing knight from his horse. The knights charged at each other on horseback down narrow lanes, called lists. Although the knights were not trying to kill each other, the tilting competition was a test of bravery and skill, and sometimes resulted in serious injury.

CASTLES

IN MEDIEVAL times, a castle was a fortified building that served as a home for the king or a lord. Many castles also had dungeons, an armory (the place where weapons were kept), and a treasure house, as well as quarters for soldiers. Wars broke out frequently in medieval Europe, so it was important that a king or lord could protect himself, his family and followers. The castle became an important part of the feudal system *(see pages 18–19)*.

Castles were often built on hilltops to provide natural defenses. The Norman invaders of Engand built castles with strong defensive walls and moats. Inside the walls was a central stronghold called a keep.

LIFE IN A CASTLE

The keep not only provided the strongest defensive position in times of attack, it was also where the lord, his family, and followers lived. Inside was a great hall, where everyone ate. Servants carried food from the kitchens nearby. The hall was lit by candles and by torches made of wood and fat. Although there was a large fireplace for a fire to warm the hall, there was no glass in the windows, and most castles were cold and drafty places. At night the lord and lady would retire to their private apartment, known as a *solar*, but followers and servants simply rolled themselves in their cloaks and slept on the straw-covered floor, together with the castle's domestic animals.

KEY
1 *Keep*
2 *Crenellations in outer walls*
3 *Portcullis*
4 *Drawbridge*

A castle under attack. The castle's soldiers fire arrows at the enemy below from their powerful crossbows. The enemy are using various machines to attack a castle. They include a trebuchet, a machine that catapults rocks into the castle; a belfry, a tower from which attackers can climb into the castle; and a battering ram, a tree trunk that is swung against the castle gates. Sometimes an enemy laid siege to a castle, waiting until its occupants starved.

This castle *(below)* has a moat, a strong outer wall, a drawbridge, and a portcullis. For extra protection, its outer wall has jagged tops, called crenellations. The strong tower inside the walls is the keep. There are also cottages where staff and animals live.

ATTACKING A CASTLE

The outer wall of a castle was often surrounded by a water-filled moat. A drawbridge across the moat could be pulled up if the castle was attacked. The main entrance was also protected by a portcullis (an iron grating). The outer walls were usually topped with crenellations, allowing defenders to fire arrows while remaining under cover. There were also narrow slits in the walls through which archers fired.

CRUSADER CASTLES

The crusaders built castles in the Holy Land to defend land that they managed to take from the Turks *(see pages 22–23)*. The design of these castles copied ideas from Byzantine fortresses, with additional defensive walls within the main wall. The best-known crusader castle is Krak des Chevaliers in present-day Syria. It was built by the Knights of St. John in the 1100s.

AFRICA

AFRICA was home to a wide variety of peoples and cultures, including civilizations to rival anything known in medieval Europe. However, knowledge of much of African history is sketchy because of the scarcity of any written records. Much of what we do know comes from archaeological records—the physical remains, such as ruins, of ancient peoples.

THE BANTU MIGRATIONS

Bantu is the name given to a group of languages spoken by people from the Niger and Congo regions of West Africa. Some time during the first century B.C., these peoples began to spread out to the south and east. They took with them knowledge about growing crops and working iron.

This tall, thin monument is known as a stela. It is one of the stelae erected in Aksum in northeast Africa during the time of the Kingdom of Aksum (A.D.100–700). The stelae were placed to mark the tombs of the rulers of Aksum. They were carved to look like tall, thin multi-story houses. The tallest, now fallen down, was 108.3 feet (33 m) high.

A Bantu herdsman with his cattle. In some parts of tropical Africa it was impossible to keep herds of cattle because of the presence of a blood-sucking insect called the tsetse fly. This fly passed on a disease called sleeping sickness which killed both cattle and humans.

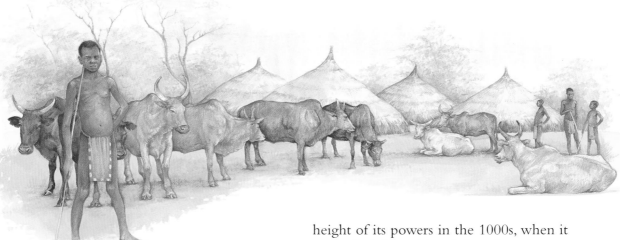

THE SPREAD OF ISLAM

Within only a century of the death of the prophet Muhammad in 632 *(see pages 4–5),* Islam had taken a firm hold in northern Africa. The Islamic faith traveled across the vast Sahara with traders, who made the hazardous journey through the desert in camel caravans. They traded with the ancient Kingdom of Ghana (in present-day Mali and Mauritania). Ghana reached the height of its powers in the 1000s, when it controlled the gold and the salt trade across the western Sahara. However, Ghana declined as the state of Mali became increasingly powerful and took over the control of trans-Saharan trade. The rulers of Mali were mostly Muslim, the most famous being Mansa Musa, who in 1324–25 went on a lavish piligrimage to the Muslim holy city, Mecca *(see page 4).* As he travelled with 60,000 followers, Mansa Musa gave away vast quantities of gold. His fame spread as far away as Europe.

Great Zimbabwe was the capital of a large state that thrived in south-eastern Africa between 1300 and 1450. Great Zimbabwe grew powerful through trade, acting as the middleman between the gold-producing states to the west and the Swahili traders on the eastern coast. The Shona people of Great Zimbabwe were also cattle-herders, and they sited their capital in an area with plentiful grazing. The word *zimbabwe* comes from Shona words meaning "stone buildings." The walls of Great Zimbabwe were skilfully made and in some places are almost a metre thick.

WEST AFRICAN STATES

Further to the south of Ghana and Mali lay other powerful states. They included Benin, Dahomey, Asante, and the Hausa city-states. Although influenced by Muslim ideas from the north, the rulers of these states continued to practice traditional religions. Some of the states became rich from gold production, for example, Asante. Many of them traded gold and ivory with Europeans after the first Portuguese ships appeared along the coast of West Africa in the 1400s. In the 1500s, the terrible trade in slaves started *(see page 40),* when African captives were taken across the Atlantic Ocean to work in the Americas.

African kings ruled over thriving kingdoms at a time when European peoples were suffering the effects of plague and war in the later Middle Ages. Their capital cities were protected by immense walls. Their lands were ruled with the help of powerful armies and by making alliances with local leaders.

EAST AFRICA

Trade in East Africa was already well-established when Muslim Arabs began to settle along the coast some time around the 1000s. Trading centers such as Kilwa, Mogadishu, and Zanzibar developed and prospered, with goods coming from as far afield as China. People spoke Swahili, and their culture became a blend of black African and Islamic traditions.

Many other kingdoms flourished in the grasslands and forests of central and south Africa, especially in places with fertile soils, and sources of salt and metals nearby.

The mosque at Jenne in Mali was built during the 14th century. It is made from clay on a timber structure. Jenne was an important city because it lay on one of the major long-distance trade routes across the Sahara.

NORTH AMERICA

BEFORE the arrival of European settlers in the 1500s, North America was home to millions of people known as Native Americans (or American Indians). The first Native Americans arrived in North America thousands of years ago and developed an extraordinary variety of life styles and cultures as they spread across the continent.

NATIVE AMERICAN TRIBES

Native Americans lived in groups called tribes. At the time of the arrival of Europeans there were about 300 different tribes, each with its own form of government, language, religious beliefs, and culture. The way of life of a tribe depended largely on the environment in which they lived. The Inuit of the frozen Arctic hunted seals for food. They used the sealskins to make shelters, boats, and clothing. But in the hot, dry southwest region of North America, the Pueblo peoples built houses

The ruins of the Cliff Palace in Mesa Verde, Colorado. This structure was built by the Anasazi people of the Southwest.

from dried mud, called adobe. Water was scarce, so they developed special techniques, often tapping water supplies deep beneath the ground.

A Native American settlement on the northeast coast of North America. This is a village of the Algonquin people who built dome-shaped shelters out of birch bark. The peoples of the northeast also used birch bark to make elegant canoes.

DAILY LIFE

Wherever a tribe lived, daily life centered around providing the necessities of life— food and shelter. The main crops grown by Native Americans included maize, squashes, and beans. Many tribes lived by hunting animals such as buffalo and game, or by gathering berries, roots and other wild plants. Shelters varied widely from tribe to tribe. Nomadic tribes built movable shelters. Great Plains tribes, for example, lived in tipis, cone-shaped tents made from buffalo skin stretched over a wooden frame (see page 47). Religion played an important part in the life of all Native Americans. They believed in a powerful spirit world which influenced the lives of all humans.

SOUTH AMERICA

MANY CIVILIZATIONS flourished in the Andes region of South America before the arrival of Europeans in the 1500s. The best known is the huge empire of the Incas, which was at its height in the late 1400s and early 1500s. But other societies, for example the Huari, Tiahuanaco and Chimu, also controlled large areas of this mountainous region at various times.

Further east, across the Andes mountains, lay the vast basin of the Amazon River, covered in tropical rain forest. This hot and humid region was home to numerous tribes of Native Americans. Many used a form of agriculture known as slash-and-burn, in which a small area of rain forest was cleared in order to grow crops. When the soil was exhausted, people moved on to a new plot, leaving the old clearing to be taken over once again by the forest.

The ruins of Machu Picchu, an Inca settlement high in the Andes.

ANDES EMPIRES

The civilization of Tiahuanaco was based near Lake Titicaca, high in the mountains of present-day Peru and Bolivia. It was at its most powerful between A.D. 500 and 1000. The Huari was at its height around A.D. 800.

It was based further north than Tiahuanaco, and it seems that the two peoples were rivals. The Chimu ran their empire from their capital at Chan Chan, on the north coast of Peru. However, the Chimu were conquered by the Incas in the 1470s. The Incas ruled from their capital, Cuzco, high in the Andes mountains. They built up a vast empire by conquest, and then set up an efficient form of government to rule their subject peoples. They built a network of roads and introduced a system of taxes to pay for the running of the empire.

An Inca procession winds its way along a road high in the Andes mountains. The Incas were great builders. They constructed a network of roads that crisscrossed their mountainous empire, building rope suspension bridges where necessary. The emperor, known as the Sapa Inca, and other important officials were carried from place to place in litters. Other people walked. Important messages were carried by teams of runners, each one running a distance of 1.24 miles (2 km) before passing the message on.

RUSSIA

THE NAME RUSSIA comes from the Viking people who arrived at the town of Novgorod in the 860s. These Vikings were known as the Varangian Rus. Some historians think that they were invited to Novgorod to sort out quarrels between the Slav peoples who lived there. Others say that the Vikings invaded. Whichever is correct, the Vikings settled in the area between Novgorod and Kiev, and it became known as the land of the Rus.

The first ruler to bring the area under his single authority was Prince Vladimir I (ruled 980–1015). He became a Christian in 988, and made Orthodox Christianity the official religion of his new state.

Ivan the Terrible ordered the building of St. Basil's Cathedral in Moscow. Work started on it in the 1550s. It was built to celebrate Ivan's victories over the Tatars (Mongol peoples) in the southeast. St. Basil's stands inside the Kremlin *(opposite)*, a fortified citadel in the center of Moscow.

MONGOL RULE

In 1223 Mongols *(see pages 14–15)* attacked Russia, nearly reaching the city of Kiev. In further attacks in 1237 the Mongols sacked the city and devastated much of the land. Russia became part of the Mongol empire, included in a region known as the Golden Horde. The Mongols forced their subjects to pay heavy taxes and in 1330 they began to entrust the task of collecting these taxes to the Prince of Moscow, Ivan I. At around the same time, the leader of the Orthodox Christian Church in Russia made Moscow his main center. Kiev declined as the power of Moscow increased.

The Mongols' control over the Golden Horde grew weaker in the 1300s. In 1380 an army led by Prince Dmitri of Moscow defeated the Mongols at Kulikovo, near the Don River. A century later (in 1480), under the rule of Ivan III, Mongol power in Russia finally came to an end. Ivan declared himself Czar of all Russia, using the Slav version of the name of the Roman emperor, Caesar. From this time, all Russian leaders were known as czars (or tsars).

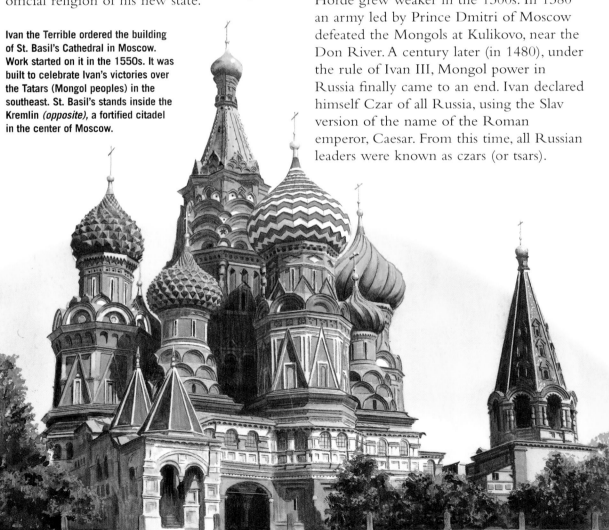

Ivan the Terrible was the grandson of Ivan III (known as Ivan the Great). He became renowned for his cruelty. During his reign of terror, he ordered the murder of anyone he considered a threat. He even killed his own son in a fit of rage in 1581.

The cossacks *(right)* were famed for their riding skills and bravery in battle. The word *cossack* means "adventurer."

IVAN THE TERRIBLE

Ivan IV (ruled 1533–84) was the first Russian ruler to be crowned czar, in 1547. The power of the new czar extended across all of Russia, and his brutality was soon being felt by many of his subjects, earning him the name "Ivan the Terrible". In 1565 Ivan set up a special police force in order to break the power of the Russian nobility. Noble landowners were thrown off their estates, and many were murdered. Ivan gave these estates to his officials. Many people fled from the area around Moscow.

After the death of Ivan the Terrible, Russia entered a period known as the Time of Troubles, when civil wars and invasions rocked the whole of Russia.

THE ROMANOVS

The Time of Troubles came to end in 1613 after the defeat of Polish invaders, and the election of Michael Romanov as the new czar. The Romanov czars were to rule Russia for the next 300 years. One of the most famous czars was Peter the Great (ruled 1682–1725). He founded the city of St. Petersburg in 1703. He also did much to reorganize the government of Russia, introducing many Western ideas.

During the rule of Catherine the Great (ruled 1762–1796) Russia's empire expanded further. But most ordinary Russians were serfs (peasants) living in terrible poverty. An uprising in the 1770s was put down by the government with great severity. Afterwards, Catherine increased control over the serfs.

VOYAGES OF EXPLORATION

IN 1492 Christopher Columbus (1451–1506) sailed west across the Atlantic Ocean. His aim was to find a sea route to the rich lands of the Far East—the lands of spices and silks. These lands were known to Europeans as the Indies. When Columbus set foot on one of the Caribbean islands he was convinced that he had found the Indies. He called the local people that he met Indians. To this day, the Caribbean islands are known as the West Indies.

HENRY THE NAVIGATOR

Prince Henry of Portugal, known as Henry the Navigator, played a large part in directing Portuguese exploration in the 1400s. The Portuguese designed a new type of ship called the caravel, which could withstand the ocean waves, and was very easy to maneuver. Instruments such as the astrolabe also helped sailors to find their way with more accuracy.

Columbus's fleet was made up of three ships, the *Niña*, the *Pinta* and the *Santa Maria*. He made three later voyages, exploring the Caribbean coasts of Central and South America.

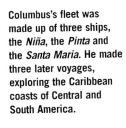

TRADE ROUTES

Luxury goods such as jewels, silks and spices had long been imported into Europe from the East along the Silk Road *(see page 8)*. But such overland routes had fallen under control of the Turks. In the 1400s both the Portuguese and the Spanish became interested in finding an alternative sea route to the riches of the East.

PORTUGUESE VOYAGES

Between 1424 and 1434 Prince Henry the Navigator sent many expeditions to explore the west coast of Africa. He wanted to find the source of the gold that was brought by Muslim traders north across the Sahara *(see page 26)*. In 1487 a Portuguese sailor called Bartholomeu Dias became the first European to sail around the southernmost tip of Africa, the Cape of Good Hope. He turned back soon after rounding the cape, and arrived back in Portugal in 1488. Ten years later, Vasco da Gama went even further. He sailed around the Cape of Good Hope, up the east coast of Africa and reached India in 1498. He made a second voyage in 1502.

The Chinese explorer Zheng He made seven expeditions between 1405 and 1433. He explored as far as the east coast of Africa in a junk, a Chinese ship.

In 1519 five ships set sail from Spain. They were commanded by Ferdinand Magellan. He planned to sail down the coast of South America and round its southern-most tip. His aim was to sail west to find a route to the Spice Islands in the Far East, for the eastwards route around Africa was forbidden to Spanish ships. In fact, Magellan's fleet became the first to sail right around the world, although Magellan himself was killed in the Philippines.

THE NEW WORLD

The Italian sailor Christopher Columbus tried to persuade the Portuguese to pay for a voyage across the Atlantic Ocean, but they refused. Eventually his 1492 voyage was sponsored by Queen Isabella of Spain. The Spanish were very excited by Columbus's discovery, and they paid for three more voyages under his command. European interest in the New World was to have a terrible outcome for the native peoples of the Americas *(see pages 46-47)*.

Other sailors also set out to explore this "new world." Another Italian, John Cabot, sailing in the service of the English king Henry VII, reached the coast of North America in 1497. Amerigo Vespucci sailed to South America in 1499 and again in 1501. A German mapmaker wrote a version of his first name, Amerigo, on an early map of the new continent, giving us the name America.

Spanish invaders, known as conquistadors (conquerors) arrive in the Americas. Two famous conquistadors were Hernan Cortés (1485–1547) and Francisco Pizarro (1475–1541). Cortés conquered the Aztec empire *(see page 11)*, while the Inca empire *(see page 29)* fell to Pizarro. The Spanish claimed the New World for themselves and quickly established colonies there, often using brutal force. The local peoples were forced to work on their plantations. The Spanish also brought with them European diseases, such as smallpox, that were previously unknown to the local peoples. Native Americans had no immunity to these diseases, and epidemics swept through their populations, killing many thousands.

RENAISSANCE

THE WORD *renaissance* means "rebirth" and it describes a time when the arts and learning of ancient Greece and Rome were rediscovered by people in Europe. The Renaissance started in the 14th century in Italy, and spread across Europe during the 15th century. Many historians use the Renaissance to mark the end of the Middle Ages in Europe. It was a time when people started to think about themselves, and the world around them, in a new way.

BEGINNINGS

Italy in the 1300s was not the unified country that it is today. It was made up of many city-states which were controlled by powerful families, such as the Gonzaga family in Mantua. These wealthy families employed architects to design grand buildings that echoed the classical designs of ancient Greece and Rome, and artists to decorate them. They also encouraged scholars to study the works of ancient Greek and Roman writers.

During the 1400s the Medici family rose to power in Florence and made the city an important center for the Renaissance. Venice became another leading center.

Saint Catherine of Alexandria by Raphael (1483–1520)

HUMANISM

Renaissance scholars were interested in the study of human nature. This was known as humanism. They read texts about the great civilizations of Greece and Rome that had long been forgotten. The study of humanism was boosted when many scholars fled west from Constantinople in 1453 *(see page 7),* bringing with them many precious books.

The Renaissance started in the cities of northern Italy. Wealthy families paid for buildings designed in the classical style.

The first stone of St. Peter's in Rome was laid by Pope Julius II in 1506. Some of the greatest architects of the Renaissance played a part in its design. They included Bramante, Michelangelo, and Bernini, who designed the magnificent *baldacchino* (canopy) that towers over the main altar. Michelangelo designed the huge 433-foot (132-m) high dome, although it was not completed until after his death.

WRITERS AND ARTISTS

In literature, some of the first writers to use humanism in their work were the Italian poets Dante and Petrarch. Humanism also had a major influence on styles of painting. In the Middle Ages, artists painted in a flat, decorative style. They were not concerned with making their figures look natural. The Florentine painter Giotto became the first artist to try to portray figures in a lifelike way. Later in the Renaissance, artists such as Leonardo da Vinci, Michelangelo, and Raphael worked for rich patrons in Rome and elsewhere. Michelangelo's best-known work is the ceiling of the Sistine Chapel in the Vatican in Rome. Leonardo da Vinci was fascinated by the natural world and particularly by the human body.

Galileo Galilei (1564–1642), the great Italian astronomer.

NEW HORIZONS

As well as being a period of new ideas in the arts, the Renaissance was also a time for new inventions and discoveries. The 1400s was a time of exploration, when continents previously unknown to Europeans were discovered. In astronomy, Nicolaus

Leonardo da Vinci (1452-1519) was a painter, scientist and engineer: a "Renaissance Man". This design for a rotor was made in about 1500.

Copernicus, a Polish astronomer, declared the idea that the Earth orbited the Sun (and not the other way round as previously thought). Inventions such as the sailor's compass, gunpowder and printing also revolutionized life for many people.

REFORMATION

ON October 31, 1517 a German monk named Martin Luther nailed a document to the door of the Castle Church in Wittenberg. The document, known as the Ninety-five Theses, contained a series of attacks on the corruption of the Roman Catholic Church. Luther's act of protest marked the beginning of a religious movement called the Reformation.

A soldier in the Thirty Years' War (1618–1648), a conflict between Protestant and Catholic states in Europe.

CHURCH CORRUPTION

By the time of the Renaissance *(see pages 34–35),* the Roman Catholic Church was extremely powerful throughout Europe. Its center was in Rome, where the pope and his court lived in lavish style. Many people thought that the church had become corrupt, for example in its practices of offering important positions within the church, or of selling "indulgences" (pardons from sins), for money. These abuses were attacked by humanist scholars such as the Dutch priest, Desiderius Erasmus. But it was Luther's protest that started the process that eventually led to a split in the Roman Catholic Church.

Although Luther had no intention of breaking with the Catholic Church when he first demanded his reforms, he was excommunicated (thrown out) of the church by the pope in 1521. Nevertheless, he received support for his reforms from some rulers in Germany. It was during this time that the word *Protestant* began to be used to describe those "protesting" against the Catholic Church. The Protestant movement spread across Germany, and into Sweden and Denmark. In Switzerland it was taken up by a priest called Ulrich Zwingli who worked in Zürich.

Martin Luther posts his Ninety-five Theses on the door of the Castle Church in Wittenberg. He believed that people were saved by faith alone.

The Escorial in Spain was built by Philip II, a supporter of the Counter-Reformation.

Another reformer, called John Calvin, lived in Geneva in Switzerland. He worked to establish Protestantism in France, where his followers became known as Huguenots. Calvin's teachings spread to Scotland through the preaching of John Knox.

THE ANGLICAN CHURCH

England broke with the Catholic Church for its own reasons. King Henry VIII wished to divorce his first wife, Catherine of Aragon. When the pope refused to grant the divorce, Henry broke with the church in 1534, having already become the head of the church in England in 1531. Later, during the reign of Edward VI, the Protestant church in England became known as the Anglican Church.

COUNTER-REFORMATION

As Protestantism spread across Europe, the Catholic Church began to fight back with a movement known as the Counter-Reformation. There was reform within the church, and many of the old abuses were wiped out. Catholic priests went out among the people and campaigned against Protestantism. The Catholic Church still remained very powerful, particularly in Spain and Italy. But the split between Catholics and Protestants in Europe led to persecution and conflict. In 1572 thousands of Huguenots were murdered by French Catholics in the St. Bartholomew's Day Massacre. Religious wars continued during the following centuries.

A Spanish war galleon of the 16th century. England and Spain went to war in 1588, when Spain, under Philip II, attempted to invade England. But the Spanish Armada (fleet) was wrecked by storms around Britain.

ISLAMIC EMPIRES

IN 1453 the Ottoman Turks captured Constantinople. This was the final stage in the Ottoman conquest of the Byzantine Empire *(see page 7),* and Constantinople, renamed Istanbul, became the centre of a wealthy and glittering Islamic empire.

The Ottoman Turks originally settled in Anatolia (present-day Turkey) in the 1200s. They gradually conquered the surrounding territories, building up a vast empire. By the 1600s, the Ottoman Empire was the largest in the world, covering much of eastern Europe, North Africa and the Middle East.

The name *Ottoman* comes from Osman, the first sultan (ruler) of the empire. One of the most famous of the Ottoman sultans was Süleyman I, known as Süleyman the Lawgiver, or the Magnificent (ruled 1520–66). Süleyman expanded his empire and made it into a power to be feared and respected. Craft work, literature, education, and architecture flourished during his reign.

THE SAFAVIDS

The Safavids were another Turkish people. Under their leader Ismail I, they gained power in Persia in the 1500s. Ismail became the first shah (ruler) of the Safavid dynasty.

The Ottoman sultans lived in magnificent luxury in the Topkapi Palace in Istanbul, the capital of their vast empire.

The most famous of the Safavid rulers was Shah Abbas (ruled 1587–1629). Under his leadership, the Safavid army defeated the Ottomans and recaptured land lost in earlier wars. Shah Abbas made his capital at Isfahan, and encouraged study of the arts and architecture. After his death, the Safavid empire began to decline, and it was overrun by armies from Afghanistan in 1722.

The Royal Mosque in the city of Isfahan, in Persia (present-day Iran). Building work on the magnificent Royal Mosque and the Lotfollah Mosque was started during the reign of Shah Abbas, although the Royal Mosque was not completed until after his death. At the height of the Safavid empire—during the 17th century—the city of Isfahan was renowned all over the world for its beauty. Situated high on a barren plain, it had tree-lined avenues, 162 mosques, and 273 public baths.

MUGHAL INDIA

The Mughal empire was founded in 1526, with the victory of Babur, a ruler from Afghanistan, at the Battle of Panipat. Babur could trace his ancestry back to Tamerlane and Genghis Khan *(see pages 14-15)*. He became the first of the six Great Mughals who ruled over an empire that stretched across almost the whole of India. The Mughal rulers were Muslims, while the majority of their subjects were Hindus.

Babur's grandson, Akbar, is considered to be the greatest of the Mughal emperors. He came to power in 1556 when he was only 13 years old. He set up a system of government and tolerated all religions.

Dancers performing at the court of the great Mughal emperors. The Mughals built magnificent palaces, surrounded by beautiful gardens where they could take refuge from the summer heat. Water played an important part in Mughal gardens, cascading down formal terraces, or gushing into pools.

The Taj Mahal *(above)* lies on the banks of the Yamuna River near Agra, India. It was built by Shah Jahan *(left)* as a tomb for his wife, Mumtaz. Work on the tomb started in 1632 and continued for 22 years. It was designed by Isa Khan, a Persian architect.

Akbar's son, Jahangir, succeeded after his death in 1605. During this time the Mughal empire was at the height of its powers. Shah Jahan (ruled 1628–58) and Aurangzeb (ruled 1658–1707) succeeded as emperors, but after Aurangzeb's death the empire declined, and parts of it came under British rule.

COLONIES AND COMMERCE

THE VOYAGES of exploration of the 16th century *(see pages 32–33)* opened up new possibilities to countries in Europe. Spain and Portugal began to establish colonies and trading posts in the lands discovered by their sailors. Spain took control of large areas of land in the Caribbean, as well as Central and South America. Portugal set up trading posts along the coasts of Africa and India. They were soon joined by Holland, France, and Britain, who also began to lay claim to trading ports and other possessions overseas.

Black African captives were often chained together and forced to walk to the slave ports on the west African coast.

The Spanish colonists planted sugarcane plants in plantations, where they forced the local Indians to work. But so many of the local people died from ill-treatment and from disease epidemics *(see page 33)* that there was soon a shortage of laborers. In the early 1500s the first captives were brought from Africa to the Americas to work as slaves on plantations. The trickle soon turned to a flood, as thousands of people were shipped across the Atlantic Ocean. Many died on the journey from the terrible conditions on board ship.

Founded by the Dutch, the settlement of New Amsterdam was taken over by the British in 1664 and renamed New York.

THE SLAVE TRADE

Spanish colonists in the Caribbean quickly discovered that sugar cane grew well in the hot, humid climate of the islands. Sugar was a increasingly popular in Europe, particularly as it could be used to sweeten the new drinks that were also arriving from overseas colonies—coffee, tea and cocoa.

WEALTH AND PROFIT

Overseas colonies brought huge wealth to countries in Europe. Spain plundered its colonies on the American mainland, importing vast amounts of gold and silver. Portugal, too, had rich sources of gold in its colony in Brazil. Goods such as sugar from the Caribbean, tea from China, coffee and chocolate from South America also became increasingly popular across Europe.

The slave trade was another source of vast wealth. The slave trade between Africa and America is known as the triangular trade because it was made up of three stages. Ships sailed to Africa from Europe loaded with goods to exchange for slaves—guns and alcohol, for example. Captives were then transported across the Atlantic. In the Caribbean, the captives were sold and the money was used to buy sugar, rum, and tobacco which was then taken back to Europe. Britain became one of the leaders of the slave trade, but other European countries such as France, Holland, and Portugal also took part in this terrible trade. In Britain, the ports of London, Liverpool, and Bristol flourished as the profits poured in.

Pirates attack a treasure-carrying Spanish galleon in the Caribbean Sea in the 1600s.

TRADE WITH CHINA

Although the Chinese were happy to export goods such as silks and spices to the West, they rigorously controlled imports into their country. Foreigners were allowed to trade through one port only, Guangzhou.

World trade received a boost with the opening of the Suez Canal in 1869. The canal created a shortcut between the Mediterranean Sea and the Red Sea.

The British steamship _Nemesis_ attacks Chinese junks (ships) during the Opium Wars. Opium is a drug that is made from the juice of the opium poppy. It is dangerous because it is addictive. Opium addiction was a serious problem in China in the 18th and 19th centuries.

In the 19th century British merchants in China tried to get round these restrictions by illegally importing the drug opium. They were backed by the British govern-ment, resulting in the Opium Wars between Britain and China (1839–42 and 1856–60). China was forced to back down and accept European trade in its territories.

THE AGE OF REVOLUTION

IN THE second half of the 18th century two major revolutions took place. The first was in North America (1775–1783), and it led to the birth of the United States of America. The second happened in France, starting with the storming of the Bastille (prison) in Paris in 1789.

REVOLUTION IN AMERICA

From the early 16th century onward, North America had been settled by European colonists. During the French and Indian War (also known as Seven Years' War) (1756–1763), British and French colonists fought over territory in North America.

The guillotine was the main method of execution during the French Revolution. Thousands of people suspected of being hostile to the government were beheaded during the Reign of Terror 1793–94.

Britain emerged victorious, with control of a vast area of land. By this time there were The Thirteen Colonies in North America (apart from Canada). The colonists were under British rule but had no say in how they were governed. During the years after the war, the British government imposed many different taxes on the colonists. These taxes provoked protests against what the colonists called "taxation without representation." The first shots between British troops and American colonists that were fired in Lexington, Massachusetts on April 19, 1775, marked the start of the war. In July 1776 the colonists issued the Declaration of Independence and the United States of America was born. The end of the war came in 1783, when British troops surrendered at Yorktown, Virginia.

On July 14, 1789 a Parisian mob stormed the royal prison in the capital, the Bastille. Although there were few prisoners in the prison, the storming of the prison seriously weakened the authority and power of the French king, Louis XIV. At the same time, riots broke out across the country. The French Revolution had begun. Louis XIV and his wife, Marie-Antoinette, tried to escape, but they were arrested. The National Assembly abolished the monarchy in 1792. The king was tried and executed on the guillotine in January 1793. Marie-Antoinette followed him to the guillotine in October of the same year.

A meeting of leaders of the American colonists in the Second Continental Congress in July 1775. The Congress issued the Declaration of Independence—drawn up by Thomas Jefferson—which asserted the independence of the American colonies from Britain. The Declaration was not recognized by Britain until the signing of the Treaty of Paris in 1783, marking the end of the war in which British forces were defeated by American troops commanded by George Washington.

THE FRENCH REVOLUTION

In France discontent about taxation was also growing amongst the ordinary people in the late 18th century. At that time, neither clergy nor noble families in France paid any taxes. The burden of taxation fell on working people and peasants. In 1788 a bad harvest meant that many people were close to starvation. The country was almost bankrupt as a result of costly wars and the extravagant lifestyle of the monarchy. When the king refused to listen to the demands of the people, they formed the National Assembly. At the same time, unrest was growing in the streets and on July 14, 1789 a mob attacked the royal prison in Paris, the Bastille, in Paris. This event marked the beginning of the French Revolution.

On August 26 the National Assembly made a Declaration of the Rights of Man, giving the same basic rights to all citizens, including liberty and equality. Soon, France was also at war with many other European nations. A general called Napoleon Bonaparte had risen quickly through the ranks of the French army. In 1799 he seized power in France and began his campaign to conquer the rest of Europe.

One of the many battles of the Napoleonic Wars (1799–1815). Napoleon built an empire which covered much of Europe by 1812. He was finally defeated at the Battle of Waterloo in June 1815.

THE INDUSTRIAL REVOLUTION

THE INDUSTRIAL Revolution is the name given to a series of changes that took place in the late 18th and 19th centuries. The Industrial Revolution began in Britain, but during the 19th century it quickly spread to other European countries and to North America.

Up until the mid-1700s, most manufacturing was carried out on a small scale in people's homes or in small workshops. Machines were driven by hand, or sometimes by water- or animal-power. In the 18th century, new and bigger machines were invented making it possible to produce goods more quickly and efficiently. These new machines needed more power than could be provided by animals or water. The development of the steam engine answered this need. This new machinery was too big for homes or workshops, so manufacturing moved into mills and factories.

The Iron Bridge in Coalbrookdale, Shropshire, England, was the first bridge in the world to be made out of iron. It crosses the Severn River and was completed in 1779. Coalbrookdale was one of the main centers of iron production in the Industrial Revolution.

An industrial scene in the 19th century. Goods were transported by canal and, after the late 1820s, by railway. The new mills and factories needed supplies of coal to drive their steam engines, as well as supplies of raw materials to manufacture their goods, textiles, for example.

Children worked in the mines, cutting coal and transporting it to the surface.

COAL AND IRON

One of the reasons the Industrial Revolution developed rapidly in Britain was that there were plentiful supplies of coal and iron. Coal heated the furnaces where iron was separated from its ore in a process called smelting. It also provided fuel for steam engines. Iron was used to make engines and machines, as well as bridges and railways. As industry grew, it became vital to be able to transport goods around the country. This resulted in a period of canal-building, followed by the development of the railways.

A NEW LIFE

The Industrial Revolution caused great changes in the way people lived and worked. Millions of people moved from rural areas to work in the new factories, mills, and mines. However, in some places working conditions were appalling and dangerous. Women and children worked long hours for little pay. Housing in the new industrial centers was often overcrowded and unsanitary. Under pressure from the workers and reformers, the government eventually passed laws which aimed to improve workers' conditions.

THE SPREAD OF INDUSTRY

The process of industrialization spread rapidly across Europe in the 19th century, particularly in Belgium, France, and Germany. It reached the United States in the middle of the 19th century, and countries such as Japan later in the century.

Shipbuilding *(left)* boomed during the Industrial Revolution. Steamships with iron hulls and screw propellers were used to transport raw materials and other goods around the world. The first ship of this kind, the *Great Britain*, was launched in 1843.

A new railway in Japan *(above)*. Japan became an industrialized country in the late 19th century.

A paper mill in Britain in 1854 *(below)*. Equipped with coal-powered steam engines, mills manufactured goods such as paper and cloth.

NATIVE AMERICANS

WHEN the first Europeans arrived in North America in the 16th century, they found the land occupied by tribes of Native Americans. These local people had lived there for generations, developing their own cultures and ways of life *(see page 28)*. The arrival of Europeans changed the Native Americans' lives forever. Imported diseases *(see page 33)* spread like wildfire through the native peoples, killing millions. Many more were killed in land disputes with the European colonists.

During the 19th century European settlers poured into the United States, and the country expanded westwards *(see pages 48–49)*. At first, the American government set aside some areas of land, known as reservations, for the Native Americans. Then in 1830, the government passed the Indian Removal Act which gave it the right to force Native Americans to move from their homelands to land in the West that the European settlers did not want.

Warriors of the Sioux tribe prepared for battle by dancing together to draw on the power of the Great Spirit *(below)*. Many warriors painted an image of a powerful beast on to their shields to strengthen themselves for battle.

Sioux chiefs, such as Sitting Bull *(above)*, wore impressive eagle-feather headdresses as a sign of their great bravery. Sitting Bull was the leader of the Sioux at the time of their victory at the Battle of Little Bighorn. He was killed by American troops in 1890.

The people of the Great Plains lived in tipis, tents made from buffalo hides stretched over wooden poles. After Europeans introduced the horse into North America in the 16th century, the Native Americans of the Plains became skilful riders, using horses to help them hunt the herds of buffalo that lived on the Plains. Buffalo provided the Plains peoples with meat for food, as well as hides for clothing and shelter. When the herds of buffalo were destroyed in the 19th century, the Native Americans' way of life was destroyed, too.

FIGHTING FOR THE LAND

Most Native Americans did not want to move from their traditional homelands and fought bitterly against the American government. In the southeast, for example, the Cherokee were forced off their lands by government troops and forced to walk over 1,000 miles to reservations in the West. Thousands died, and this journey became known as the Trail of Tears. The Native Americans of the Plains also fought the settlers who moved into their territories. But their old ways of life were destroyed when hunters almost completely wiped out the herds of buffalo that lived on the Great Plains. Sometimes, Native Americans were victorious over the U.S. Army—for example, at the Battle of the Little Bighorn (1876), when Sioux warriors defeated General Custer's troops.

THE GROWTH OF AMERICA

WHEN European colonists arrived in North America in the 16th century, they founded settlements along the east coast. But after the end of the French and Indian War (see page 42), settlers began to move west of the Appalachian Mountains. These early pioneers were often fur traders, or farmers looking for new, free land.

THE OREGON TRAIL

In the 1840s the United States gained control of Oregon on the northwest coast. It also acquired New Mexico following victory in a war with Mexico. The possibility of starting a new life in the West encouraged many people to set out on the dangerous journey westwards. Many took the Oregon Trail, which started at the Missouri River and ended in the lush Willamette Valley. The journey was very hazardous, and many died.

When traveling along the Oregon or California trails, pioneers set out in groups of wagons known as wagon trains. This was for safety in case of Native American attack. At night, when the wagons stopped, they were drawn up to form a ring, called a corral, for protection. Tents were pitched inside. The women prepared food for an evening meal, while the men made repairs to the wagons and tended to the animals.

The movement westwards continued over the following decades. Then, in 1803, President Jefferson bought the vast territory of Louisiana from the French government. Louisiana stretched from the Mississippi River to the Rocky Mountains. Jefferson sent out an expedition, led by Meriwether Lewis and William Clark, to discover more about his purchase. In 1805 the expedition reached the west coast of America.

The pioneers who set out along the Oregon and California trails packed their supplies and their belongings into wagons. These wagons were wooden, with iron tires and a canvas covering. Water was stored in a barrel strapped to one side. They were pulled by teams of oxen.

Abraham Lincoln was president of the United States from 1861–1865, during the Civil War. He helped to bring an end to slavery.

THE HOMESTEAD ACT

By 1850 American settlers had reached the Mississippi River. In the west, farmers were beginning to move into Oregon and California. But much of the central part of the country, the Great Plains, remained unsettled. In 1862 the government passed the Homestead Act, which encouraged people to move there and farm the land. At the same time, the railway was being built across the continent. All of this spelled disaster for the Native Americans *(see pages 46–47)*.

Jewish refugees arrive in New York City *(right)*. Between 1840 and 1930, millions of people immigrated to the United States from all over Europe. They included Irish and Germans and, after 1890, Italians, and Jews fleeing persecution in Russia.

Bandits hold up a train in the American West *(below)*. Outlaw gangs roamed the West in the second half of the 19th century and trains were frequent targets. The first railway to link the east coast cities of America with the Pacific Coast was completed in 1869.

THE GOLD RUSH

In January 1848 a man called James Marshall was inspecting his employer's sawmill when he noticed something glittering in the water of the millstream. He picked it up. It was gold! The news of the discovery of gold in California soon leaked out. People came from all parts of America, and many parts of the world, to seek their fortunes in the goldfields of the West. Some traveled overland across the continent; others came by sea to San Francisco. Very few made any money.

WORLD EXPLORATION

IN 1768 a ship called the *Endeavour* sailed from England. It was commanded by Lieutenant (later Captain) James Cook (1728–1779). The *Endeavour* was on a scientific voyage, bound for Tahiti in the Pacific Ocean. But Cook had other instructions as well. At this time, European knowledge of the South Pacific was based on vague reports, mostly from Dutch sailors. Cook was to explore further. In fact, this was to be the first of three great voyages made by Cook, in which he charted much of the coastline of Australia and New Zealand, as well as many Pacific islands. He also sailed farther south than anyone had before him.

The Frenchman, René Caillié (1799–1838), was the first European to go to Timbuktu in Africa and return safely. Traveling disguised as an Arab, he reached Timbuktu in 1828 after a journey of about 1,500 miles (2,400 km), mostly on foot. A trading town on the southern edge of the Sahara, Timbuktu was part of the Islamic world and closed to Europeans. On his return home, Caillié was awarded a prize of 10,000 francs by the Geographical Society of Paris.

Henry Stanley was an American journalist who went to Africa to seek fame and fortune—which he did when he "found" the British explorer David Livingstone in 1871.

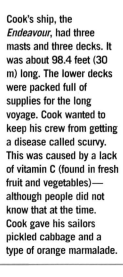

Cook's ship, the *Endeavour*, had three masts and three decks. It was about 98.4 feet (30 m) long. The lower decks were packed full of supplies for the long voyage. Cook wanted to keep his crew from getting a disease called scurvy. This was caused by a lack of vitamin C (found in fresh fruit and vegetables)—although people did not know that at the time. Cook gave his sailors pickled cabbage and a type of orange marmalade.

INTO AFRICA

During the 18th and 19th centuries European and American explorers ventured into parts of Africa never before visited by white people. They wanted to learn about the geography and people of Africa—as well as what raw materials could be obtained. They also wanted to find new markets for European goods.

Robert Peary (1856–1920) spent time with the Inuit people of Greenland, learning about methods of survival in the harsh Arctic conditions. He used husky dogs to pull sledges on his expeditions and wore traditional Inuit clothing.

Roald Amundsen (1872-1928, *right*) reached the South Pole on 14th December 1911 (*above*). Like Peary, Amundsen used dogs to pull his sleds. Amundsen's rival was Robert Scott, a British explorer who arrived at the South Pole some days after Amundsen. Scott and his team died on the return journey.

TO THE POLES

By the end of the 19th century there were few places on the earth that had not been explored and mapped by people. The exceptions were the North and South Poles. After many years of planning and failed attempts, the American Robert Peary reached the North Pole in 1909. The race to the South Pole was won by Norwegian Roald Amundsen in 1911.

On May 29, 1953, a New Zealander called Edmund Hillary and a Nepalese sherpa called Tenzing Norgay became the first people to stand on the top of the highest mountain in the world—Everest. Mount Everest stands 5.5 miles (8,863 m) above sea level. Hillary and Tenzing carried oxygen to help them breathe in the thin air at the top of the mountain. Worried that their oxygen might run out, they stayed on the top for only 15 minutes—just long enough to take some photographs to prove that they had made it.

EXPLORING SPACE

Exploration in the 20th century has gone beyond the earth and into space. The first person to travel through space was Russian cosmonaut Yuri Gagarin in 1961. In the following year, the Americans sent their first astronaut, John Glenn, into orbit. The space race between the countries resulted in the United States landing the first person on the Moon in 1969. Since then, unmanned probes have landed on Mars and have explored the Solar System, sending information and pictures back to Earth.

US astronaut Neil Armstrong (born 1930) became the first man to set foot on the Moon in July 1969. He traveled with two other astronauts, Edwin "Buzz" Aldrin and Michael Collins, in *Apollo 11*.

DAWN OF THE MODERN AGE

ALTHOUGH Britain had been the first to experience the Industrial Revolution *(see pages 44–45)*, other nations were quick to catch up. In the second half of the 19th and the early part of the 20th century, Germany, Russia, and the United States began to challenge British dominance in areas such as steel and textile production and shipbuilding.

As production increased in Europe and the United States, the industrialized countries looked abroad for sources of cheap raw materials, and for new markets in which to sell their manufactured goods. The wealthy nations exploited their old colonies but also looked for opportunities to acquire new colonies. Following the exploration of the interior of Africa *(see pages 50–51)*, European nations began to lay claim to large parts of the African continent. This became known as the Scramble for Africa.

For poor children in the cities, life at the beginning of the 20th century was hard, with cramped conditions and little to eat.

SCRAMBLE FOR AFRICA

In 1880 a tiny part of Africa was ruled by European nations. Only 20 years later, Europe had laid claim to the entire African continent with the exception of Ethiopia and Liberia. In 1884 a conference was held in Berlin to decide how Africa was to be divided up—but no African representatives were present to decide their own future.

People in the early 20th century found it difficult to get used to the noise and speed of new methods of transport such as the car and airplane. The engines used to power the earliest cars were developed separately by two German engineers, Gottlieb Daimler and Karl Benz in 1885. The first pneumatic (air-filled) tires were produced by a French firm, Michelin, 10 years later. The car industry grew rapidly in the United States thanks to a ready supply of oil to provide gasoline, and the introduction of mass-production techniques in car manufacturing.

INDUSTRIAL TECHNOLOGY

Industrialization during the 19th century went hand-in-hand with the invention of new technology. New inventions such as the telephone, the camera, the typewriter, and electric lighting transformed everyday life for many people. The increased production of iron and steel, and improvements in their technology, resulted in the construction of dramatic new structures such as the Eiffel Tower in Paris and the first skyscrapers in Chicago and New York City in the United States.

Methods of transport also benefited from new designs and technology. Railroads allowed ordinary people to travel farther and more cheaply than ever before. One of the greatest feats of railroad building was the construction of the Trans-Siberian Railway, which linked the Russian capital, Moscow, with Vladivostok on the Pacific Ocean. The bicycle was another invention that gave ordinary people greater freedom. The motor car started to become popular in the 1890s, but it was not until the mass production of Henry Ford's Model T in 1908 that most people could afford to buy one. In 1903 two American brothers, Orville and Wilbur Wright, made the first successful powered flight, marking the birth of the airplane—and a new form of transportation.

A busy street scene in New York City in about 1900. Horse-drawn buses ran along metal tracks laid in the roads. Motor cars were still a rare sight.

WORLD AT WAR

The Fokker plane of the so-called Red Baron was painted bright red. Baron Manfred von Richthofen was a German flying hero of World War I.

THE BEGINNING of the 20th century was a time of increasing rivalry between the European nations. Some nations joined together to form alliances, promising to help each other if they were attacked. Germany, Austria-Hungary, and Italy formed the Triple Alliance (later known as the Central Powers). Britain, France, and Russia formed the Triple Entente (later known as the Allies). However, the event that sparked off war took place in Sarajevo, Bosnia, when Archduke Franz Ferdinand, heir to the throne of Austria-Hungary, was assassinated by a Serbian protester in 1914. Austria-Hungary declared war on Serbia, prompting Russia to send troops to defend Serbia. Soon, Germany, France, and Britain had also been drawn into World War I.

The war was fought mainly on two fronts, in the west across Belgium and France, and in the east along the Russian border. In the west, the fighting soon turned into stalemate. A system of trenches was dug (bottom), stretching from the English Channel to Switzerland and battles were fought along this line. Millions of soldiers died on both sides. In 1917 the United States joined the war, helping the Allies to defeat the Central Powers in 1918.

Tanks (right) were used for the first time in World War I.

Russian revolutionaries go into action. They were called Bolsheviks, from the Russian word for "majority".

THE RUSSIAN REVOLUTION

Russia suffered some humiliating defeats at the beginning of World War I, for example at the Battle of Tannenberg in 1914, when German forces killed or captured thousands of Russian soldiers. Russia was ruled by Czar Nicholas II, a member of the Romanov dynasty *(see page 31),* but severe shortages of food and the massive war casualties led to popular unrest. In 1917 an uprising in St. Petersburg forced the czar to give up his throne. In a deliberate attempt to weaken Russia even further, Germany allowed a revolutionary called Lenin to return from exile in Switzerland. Lenin led another uprising in Russia, seizing control of the government. He then started peace talks with the Central Powers, and Russia withdrew from the war.

Adolf Hitler (1889–1945) rose to power as leader of the German Nazi Party in the 1930s. Other Fascist leaders included Mussolini in Italy and Franco in Spain.

WORLD WAR II

People called World War I the "war to end wars," but the peace treaty that was drawn up in 1918 punished Germany severely for its part in the war. This led to extreme nationalism in Germany and the rise to power of the National Socialist (Nazi) leader, Adolf Hitler, in the 1930s. In 1939 Germany invaded Poland, drawing nations across the world into war once again.

A British Spitfire plane. Spitfires fought German fighters and bombers in the Battle of Britain (1940) in World War II.

World War II was fought on battlefields all over the world. These troops are fighting in the desert of North Africa.

The war was fought between the Axis powers (Germany, Italy, and Japan) and the Allies (Britain and the Commonwealth countries, France, the Soviet Union, and the United States). Battles were fought all over the world—in the jungles of Southeast Asia, on Pacific islands, in the deserts of North Africa, and on the oceans. The war also came to European cities, as bombing raids destroyed buildings and killed many people. The war ended with the defeat of the Axis powers, but only after the dropping of nuclear bombs on the Japanese cities of Hiroshima and Nagasaki in 1945.

AFTER THE WAR

WORLD WAR II came to an end in 1945 *(see page 55)*. Millions had died and cities around the world were left in ruins. In particular, Hitler had been determined to wipe out Jewish communities in the territories he controlled, and millions had died in work camps and concentration camps. The terrible death and destruction inspired people to ensure that such a war could never happen again. In 1945, 50 nations signed the charter of the United Nations, promising to promote world peace.

Mohandas Karamchand Gandhi (1869–1948) led the Indian campaign for independence. He became known as Mahatma, meaning "Great Soul." He was a peace-loving man who led a campaign of resistance against the British, but refused to use violence. One of his most famous protests was the Salt March of 1930, when he led hundreds of people to the sea to make salt from seawater. This was in protest at the Salt Acts imposed by the British, which forced people to buy heavily taxed salt direct from the government.

The Soviet leader, Joseph Stalin *(right)*, U.S. President Roosevelt *(center)* and the British leader, Winston Churchill *(left)*, meet at the Yalta Conference in 1945 to discuss plans for after the end of war.

INDEPENDENCE

India had been a British territory since 1858. Despite Indian demands for reform and after 1917, for independence, Britain was very reluctant to let India go. After the 1920s the campaign for independence was led by Mahatma Gandhi.

It was not until after World War II that the British government finally agreed to Indian independence. However, religious matters led to terrible bloodshed. Although the majority of people in India were Hindus, there were also many Muslims who did not want to live under Hindu rule. The Muslim leader Mohammed Ali Jinnah campaigned for a separate state for Muslims,

THE COLD WAR

At the end of the war, it was clear that two countries—the United States of America and the Soviet Union—had become the world's leading powers, the "superpowers." (The Soviet Union was formed in 1922 when Russia joined with other territories under Communist rule.) After the war, Soviet leaders tried to extend Communist rule in Europe and Asia. The struggle between the Communists and the Americans was known as the Cold War.

`The Communists came to power in China in 1949, under the leadership of Mao Tse-tung *(right)*. Mao oversaw dramatic reforms in China designed to improve the economy and increase food production. Industries were brought under government control and land was taken over by cooperatives. However, many people were killed or sent into exile for criticizing Mao.

After the war, Germany was divided up between the United States, Britain, France, and the Soviet Union. The capital, Berlin, lay in the Soviet zone, but was also divided between the four powers. In 1949 three zones were joined together to form West Germany, while the Soviet zone became East Germany with a Communist government. Berlin remained divided, and in 1961 the Communists built a wall across the city to prevent people moving from East to West. The hated wall came down in 1989 *(right)*, when Communism in eastern Europe collapsed.

and the British were eventually forced to agree. In 1947 two areas in northwest and northeast India became the Muslim state of Pakistan (the northeast part is present-day Bangladesh). As people moved from one state to the other, violence broke out between the two sides: Thousands died. India became independent on August 15, 1947.

Many other former colonies also gained their independence after World War II. Many African colonies became independent peacefully—others were forced to fight for it. In South Africa, the white minority used a policy called apartheid to keep the black majority out of power. The struggle to end apartheid finally succeeded in 1994, when free elections were held and Nelson Mandela became president.

This is the same view of New York as on page 53, about 100 years later. The car has transformed life for people in the 20th century, giving them more freedom than ever before, but it has also introduced new problems. Pollution from exhaust fumes is a major problem in most cities. Air pollution is also a cause of global warming, which could affect the climate patterns of the earth.

THE MODERN WORLD

The Cold War finally came to an end in the early 1990s as Communism collapsed. Today, there continues to be a huge gap between rich and poor countries. Making sure that everyone across the globe has access to food, health, and education continues to be the major challenge for the future.

TIMELINE I

c.300 Rise of Mayan civilization in Central America.

410 Goths loot Rome.

429 Vandals invade northern Africa.

449 Angles, Saxons, and Jutes begin conquest of Britain.

455 Vandals sack Rome.

480 Gupta Empire in India overthrown.

486 Frankish kingdom founded by Clovis.

c.500–1000 Civilization of Tiahuanaco in Andes mountains of South America.

527–565 Justinian rules over Byzantine Empire.

532–563 Construction of Hagia Sophia in Constantinople.

552 Buddhism introduced into Japan.

c.570 Birth of the prophet Muhammad.

581–618 Sui dynasty rules in China.

c.600–900 Huari civilization in South America.

618–907 Tang dynasty rules in China.

632 Death of the prophet Muhammad.

c.632–700 Arab armies spread Islam throughout North Africa.

642 Arab armies defeat Sassanian Empire.

661–750 Umayyad dynasty holds power in the Islamic world.

c.700 Start of Pueblo period in northwest America.

711 Muslim armies conquer part of Spain.

718 Arab siege of Constantinople repulsed.

732 Muslim armies defeated at Battle of Poitiers.

750–1055 Abbasid dynasty holds power in the Islamic world.

c.750 Vikings begin raiding voyages in Europe.

768–814 Reign of Frankish leader, Charlemagne.

800 Charlemagne crowned emperor in Rome of Holy Roman Empire.

c.800 Height of Huari empire in South America.

c.800 Rise of Kingdom of Ghana in West Africa.

802 Khmer Kingdom founded in Cambodia.

c.850 First buildings constructed at Great Zimbabwe in southern Africa.

862 Novgorod founded by Vikings.

c.900 Construction starts on city of Angkor in Khmer Kingdom.

960–1279 Song dynasty rules in China.

c.982 Viking Erik the Red explores Greenland coast.

969 Fatimids conquer Egypt and found Cairo.

c.1000 Viking Leif Eriksson sails to North America.

c.1000–1476 Chimu civilization in South America.

1004–1013 Viking settlement established in Newfoundland, North America (possibly known as Vinland).

1014 Vikings defeated at Battle of Clontarf in Ireland.

1066 Duke William of Normandy (William I) conquers England.

1086 Compilation of the Domesday Book in England.

1095 Turks ban Christians from entering Jerusalem, and Pope Urban II calls on Christians to recapture the Holy Land.

1096–1272 Period of the Crusades.

1099 Knights of First Crusade capture Jerusalem.

1147–1149 Second Crusade.

1171 Muslim leader Saladin defeats Fatimids and conquers Egypt.

1187 Saladin defeats Crusaders and recaptures Jerusalem.

1189–1192 Third Crusade ends in failure.

1192–1333 Kamakura shogunate in Japan.

1202–1204 Fourth Crusade.

1206 Founding of Sultanate of Delhi.

1212 Children's Crusade.

1215 Mongols capture Beijing in China.

1215 King John of England signs Magna Carta.

1217–1222 Fifth Crusade.

1223 Mongols attack Russia.

1227 Death of Mongol leader Genghis Khan.

1228–1229 Sixth Crusade.

1237 Russia becomes part of the Mongol empire.

1248–1254 Seventh Crusade.

1270–1272 Eighth Crusade.

1271–1292 Marco Polo travels across Asia and the Far East.

1274 Mongol fleet defeated by Japan.

1279 Kublai Khan conquers China.

1281 Mongol fleet again defeated by Japan.

1294 Death of Mongol leader Kublai Khan.

1322–1325 Mansa Musa makes a lavish pilgrimage across Africa to Mecca.

1337–1453 Hundred Years' War fought between England and France.

1338–1573 Muromachi period in Japan; rule of Ashikaga shoguns.

1347 Black Death arrives in Europe, killing millions of people.

1380 Russian armies defeat Mongols at Battle of Kulikovo.

1386–1644 Ming dynasty rules in China.

1398 Tamerlane's troops attack Delhi, India.

c.1400–1521 Period of the Aztec empire in Mexico and Central America.

1402 Tamerlane defeats Ottomans at Battle of Ankara.

1405 Death of Tamerlane.

1405–1433 Zheng He, Chinese explorer, makes seven voyages.

1415 Portuguese capture Ceuta in Africa.

1415 Battle of Agincourt between France and England.

1424–1434 Prince Henry of Portugal, Henry the Navigator sends expeditions to explore the African coastline.

1428–1430 Joan of Arc leads French armies against England.

c.1438–1572 Inca empire established in Peru, South America.

c.1450–1600 Period in Western Europe known as the Renaissance.

1453 Constantinople falls to Turkish armies. End of the Byzantine Empire.

1453 England loses all territories in France except Calais.

1455–1485 Wars of the Roses in England.

1480 Mongol power in Russia finally comes to an end.

1487–1488 Bartholomeu Dias sails around the Cape of Good Hope.

1492 Christopher Columbus sails across the Atlantic Ocean and explores the Caribbean islands.

1498 Vasco da Gama reaches India.

TIMELINE II

1517 Martin Luther nails the Ninety-Five Theses to the door of the castle church in Wittenberg, marking the beginning of the Reformation.

1519 Charles I of Spain becomes Emperor Charles V of Holy Roman Empire.

1519–1522 Ferdinand Magellan's fleet circumnavigates the world.

1521 Aztec empire defeated by Spanish conquistadors.

1522–1560 Rule of Sulaiman I over the Ottoman Empire.

1526 Mughal empire founded by Babur at the Battle of Panipat.

1532 Francisco Pizarro begins conquest of Inca Empire in South America.

1533–1584 Reign of Ivan IV (Ivan the Terrible) in Russia.

1556–1605 Reign of Akbar the Great over the Mughal empire.

1571 Christian fleet defeats Ottoman fleet at Battle of Lepanto.

1572 Murder of thousands of French Huguenots in St. Bartholomew's Day Massacre.

1584–1613 Time of Troubles in Russia.

1587–1629 Rule of Shah Abbas over Safavids.

1588 Spanish Armada defeated off coast of Britain.

1603–1868 Tokugawa shogunate in Japan.

1618–1648 Thirty Years' War in Europe.

1628–1658 Reign of Shah Jahan over Mughal empire.

1632 Work starts on Taj Mahal in India

1644–1912 Period of Qing (Manchu) dynasty rule in China.

1658–1707 Reign of Aurangzeb, last Great Mughal, over Mughal empire.

1682–1725 Reign of Peter the Great in Russia.

1703 Peter the Great founds St. Petersburg.

1756–1763 Seven Years' War, fought between Britain and Prussia on one side and France, Russia, Austria and Sweden on the other.

1775–1783 American Revolution.

1776 Declaration of Independence: The United States of America is founded.

1762–1796 Reign of Catherine the Great in Russia.

1768 James Cook makes first voyage to the Pacific Ocean.

1789 Storming of the Bastille (prison) in Paris marks the start of the French Revolution.

1793 King Louis XIV executed in France.

1799 Napoleon seizes power in France.

1799–1815 Napoleonic Wars end in defeat for Napoleon at Waterloo.

1803 President Jefferson makes Louisiana Purchase.

1803–1805 Lewis and Clark lead expedition to west coast of America.

1839–1842, 1856–1860 Opium Wars between Britain and China.

1848 Year of revolutions in Europe.

1848 Discovery of gold in California, USA leads to gold rush.

1861–1865 American Civil War.

1862 Homestead Act encourages settlers to move to Midwest of the United States.

1868 Meiji Restoration in Japan.

1869 Completion of first railway line to cross the United States from coast to coast.

1870–1871 Franco-Prussian War.

1884 Conference in Berlin held by European nations to decide division of Africa.

1903 First powered flight made by American brothers Orville and Wilbur Wright.

1904–1905 Russo-Japanese War, in which Russia is defeated by Japan.

1911 Chinese Revolution; Sun Yatsen becomes first president of the republic.

1914–1918 World War I.

1917 Russian Revolution brings Communists to power under their leader, Lenin.

1922 Founding of the Soviet Union (USSR).

1922 Fascist leader Benito Mussolini marches on Rome and siezes power in Italy.

1929 Wall Street crash plunges world into the Great Depression.

1933 Adolf Hitler is elected German chancellor.

1936–1939 Spanish Civil War ends in victory for Fascist leader General Franco.

1939–1945 World War II.

1945 Atomic bombs are dropped by Allies on Japanese cities of Hiroshima and Nagasaki.

1945 United Nations is set up by former Allies.

1947 India becomes independent. Partition leads to formation of Muslim state of Pakistan.

1948 Mahatma Gandhi is assassinated in India.

1949 Communists come to power in China under leadership of Mao Tse-tung.

1950–1953 Korean War.

1953 Tenzing Norgay and Edmund Hillary reach the summit of Mount Everest.

1957 European Economic Community established at Treaty of Rome.

1961 Soviet cosmonaut Yuri Gagarin is first human in space.

1961 Wall built to divide East and West Berlin in Germany.

1962 Cuban Missile Crisis brings world to brink of nuclear war.

1963 Assassination of President John F. Kennedy.

1964–1976 Vietnam War.

1966–1976 Cultural Revolution in China.

1967 Six Day War in Middle East.

1968 Assassination of U.S. civil rights activist, Martin Luther King Jr.

1969 U.S. astronaut Neil Armstrong is the first man on the Moon.

1979 Establishment of Islamic Republic in Iran under Ayatollah Khomeini.

1980–1988 War between Iran and Iraq.

1986 Disastrous accident at Chernobyl nuclear power station in USSR.

1989 Chinese soldiers open fire on students in Tiananmen Square, Beijing.

1989–1990 Collapse of Communism in eastern Europe.

1990–1991 Iraq invades Kuwait, leading to outbreak of Gulf War.

1991 End of apartheid in South Africa.

1991 Break-up of Yugoslavia, leading to war between Serbia, Croatia, and Bosnia.

1992 Earth Summit held in Rio de Janeiro.

1994 Nelson Mandela becomes president of South Africa.

1997 British colony Hong Kong is returned to China.

1999 NATO allies defeat Serbia during Kosovo crisis.